AF255176

ANINTIMATENATURE

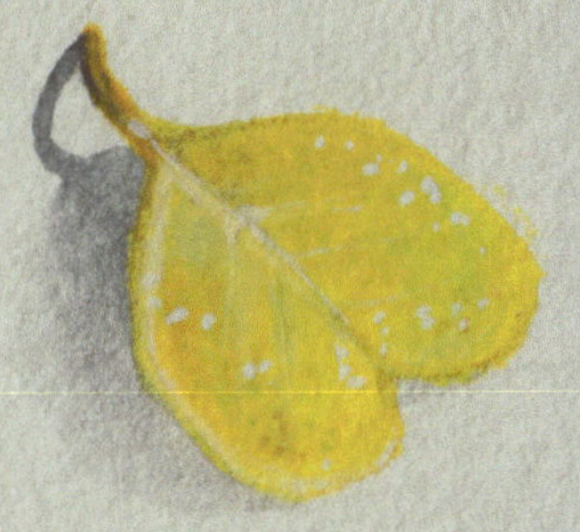

*To all the people who contributed to this book. Thank you for sharing a
small part of your journey.*

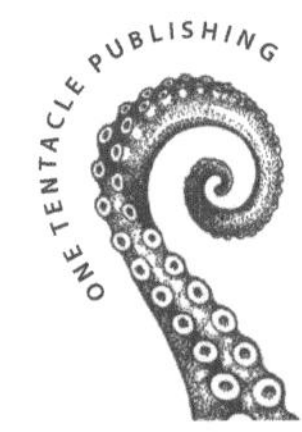

One Tentacle Publishing
PO Box 3058
Uki, New South Wales, 2484
Australia

website: www.onetentaclepublishing.com
email: onetentacle@iinet.net.au

copyright © Tina Wilson 2018
website: www.tinawilsonartist.com
Instagram: @tinawilsonartist

First published in Australia in 2018
First published in paperback 2020

All rights reserved. No part of this publication may be reproduced, stored in a retrieval system or transmitted in any form or by any means, electronic, mechanical, photocopying, recording or otherwise, without the prior written permission of the publisher.

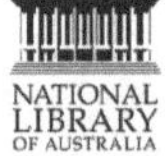

A catalogue record for this book is available from the National Library of Australia

ISBN 978 0 6485119 7 7 (pbk)

Editor: Madeleine Murray
Design & photography: Tina Wilson
Illustrations: Tina Wilson
Quotes: By members of the Uki community

ANINTIMATENATURE

A COLLECTION OF ARTWORKS BY

TINA WILSON

WITH QUOTES FROM THE UKI COMMUNITY

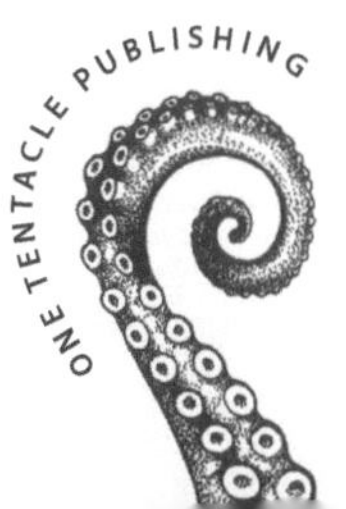

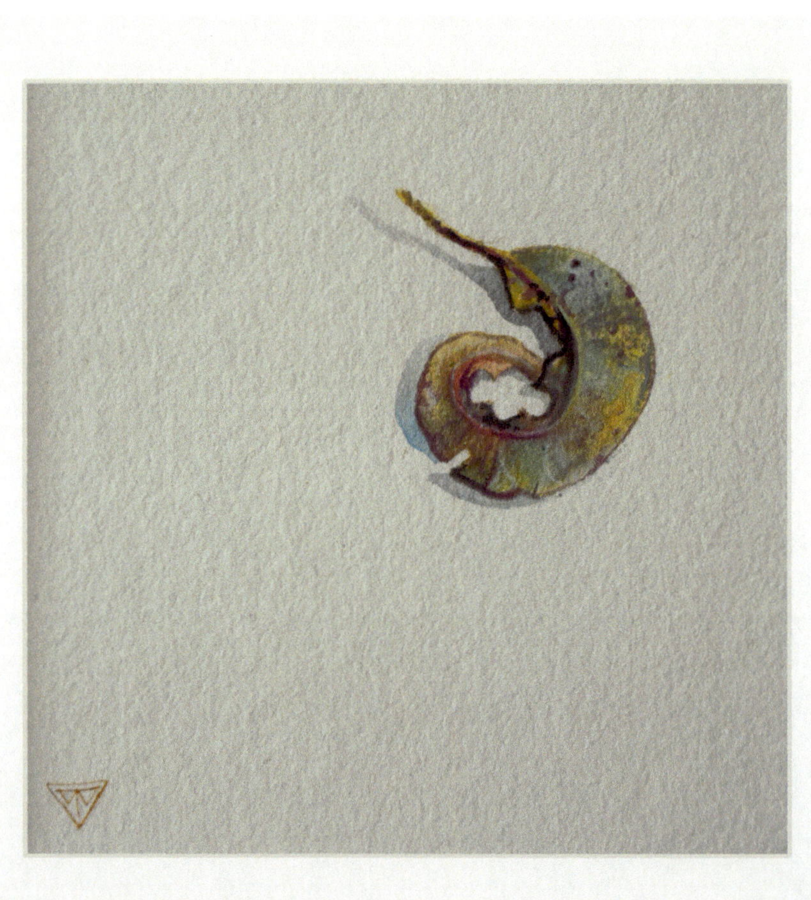

AN INTRODUCTION

When I first moved to Uki, I felt like I had come home. I found myself walking through the rainforest and reconnecting with something that I didn't realise I had lost; a sense of the quiet, of the earth and the natural world around me.

Not only have I fallen in love with the beautiful surroundings here, but also the people and the extraordinary sense of community.

I wanted this project to capture the feelings and thoughts we all share. The quotes in this book are from people that I have come to know and treasure, all whose personal journeys have brought them to this place and moment in time.

I would like to thank each of the contributors for their words of wisdom, and apologise to all those who have not had a chance to participate this time around. I look forward to working on Volume Two.

The artworks depicted in this series are all based on fallen leaves that I have found around my home. They are small, intimate works of nature, inspired by my new surrounds, a new stage in my life and a return to my roots.

TINA WILSON

Quietude
11 x 11cm
Watercolour and gouache on paper

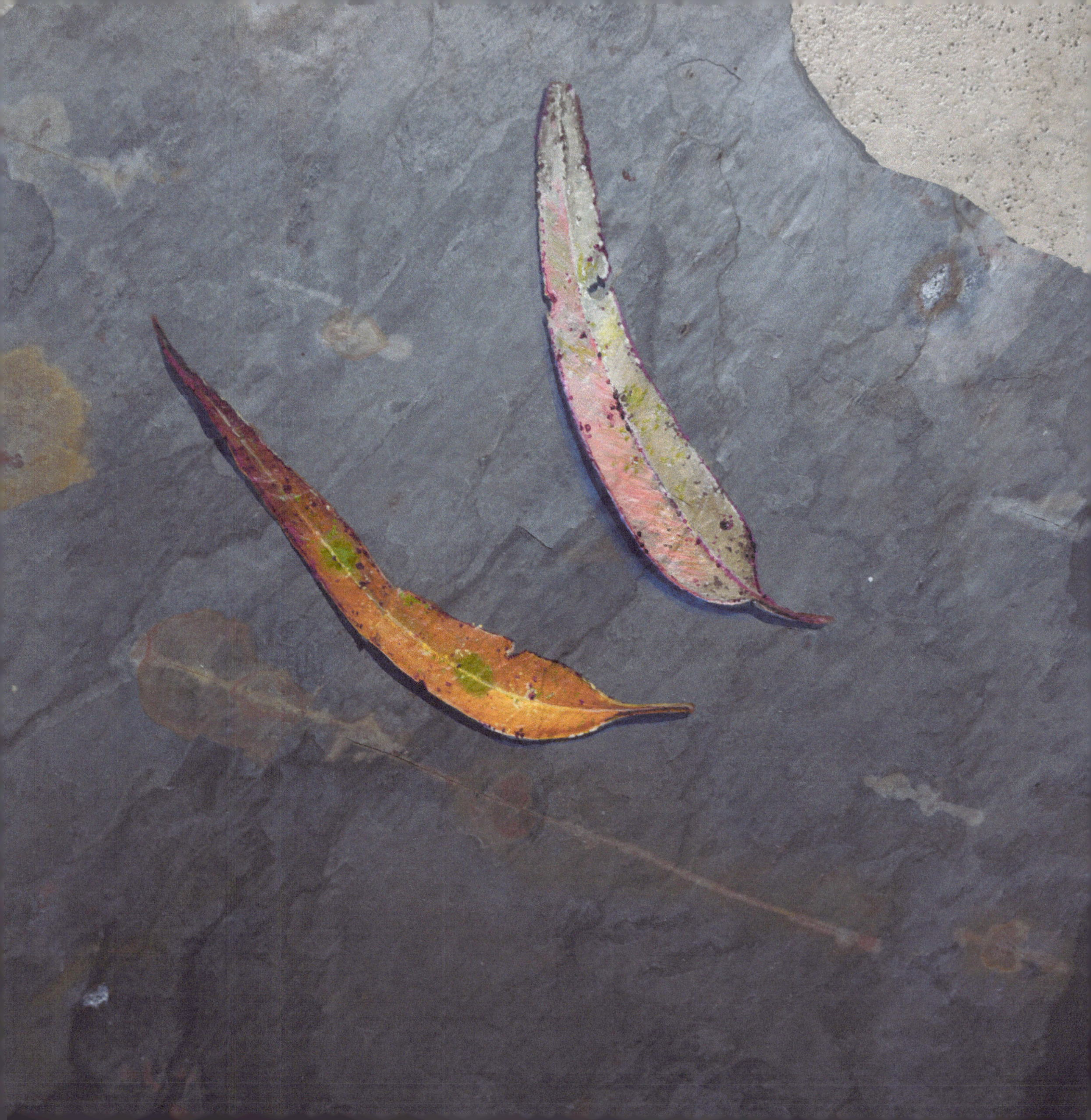

"At the least, concerning music and colour, harmony
could be thought of in terms of distance. Too close
and definition is weak bringing mutually bland
contributions to the relationship...too far and
alienation prevents recognition of any commonality.
Wilde did say, 'Life imitates art'."

Bernard Spiller

Detail from *Harmony*
29 x 29cm
Acrylic and gouache on slate

"One more day"

Jo Spiller

Detail from *Life*
18 x 15cm
Acrylic and gouache on slate

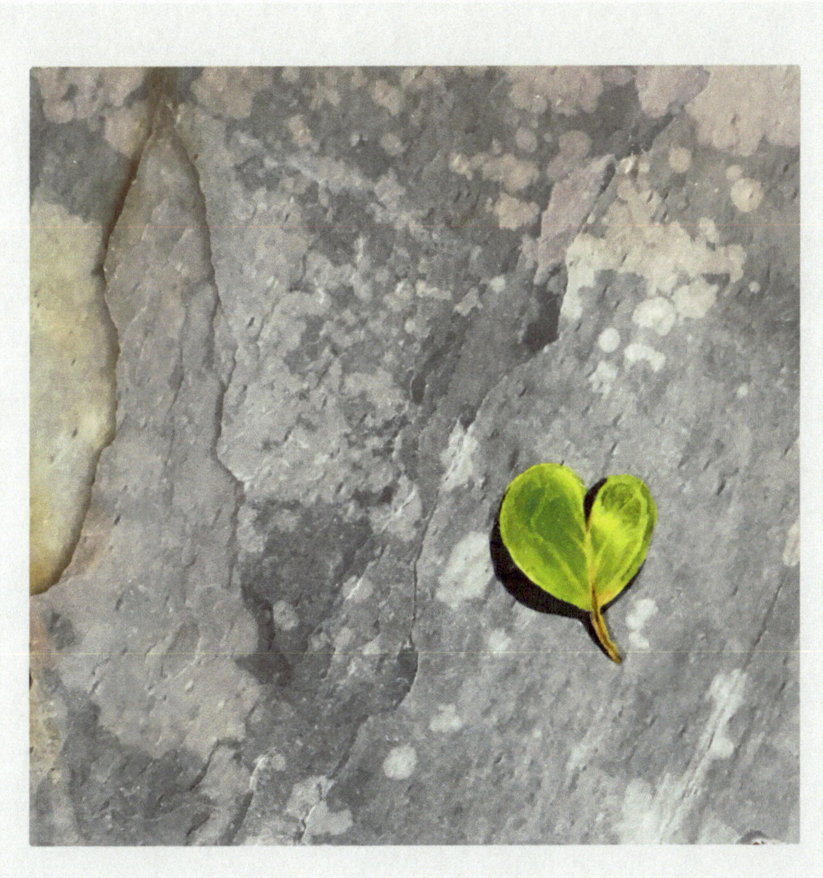

"Finding my tribe makes me feel whole. In their
reflection I make more sense."

Marlena & Pascal

Detail from *Birds of a feather*
45 x 32cm
Watercolour and gouache on paper

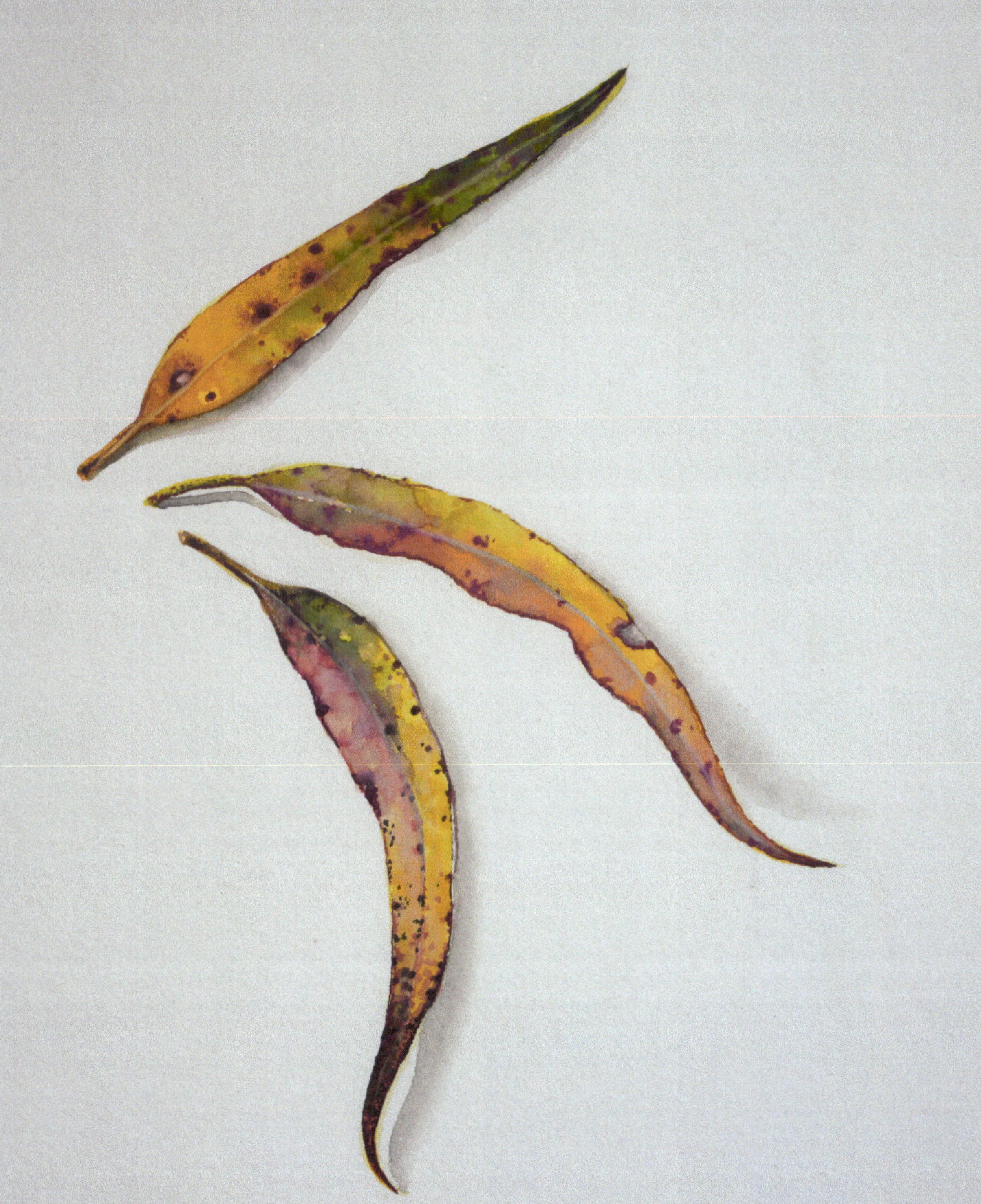

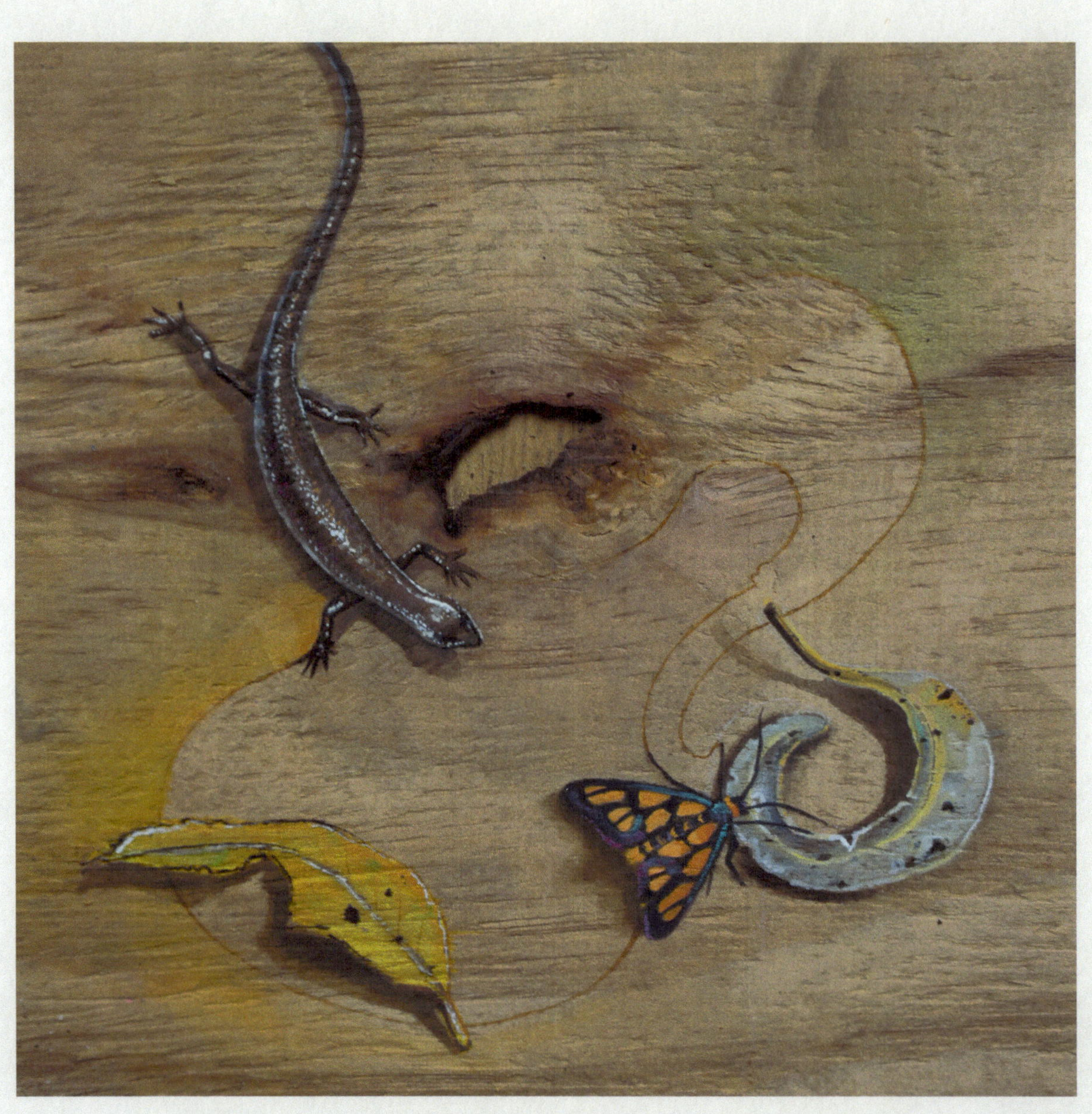

"By happy chance I noticed you there drinking tea
amongst the dregs."

Lynden Stone

Chance
17 x 17cm
Watercolour, ink and gouache on plywood

"Our thoughts become words,
our words turn into our actions,
our actions form our habits,
our habits create our character,
our character determines our destiny."

Maria Barbieri

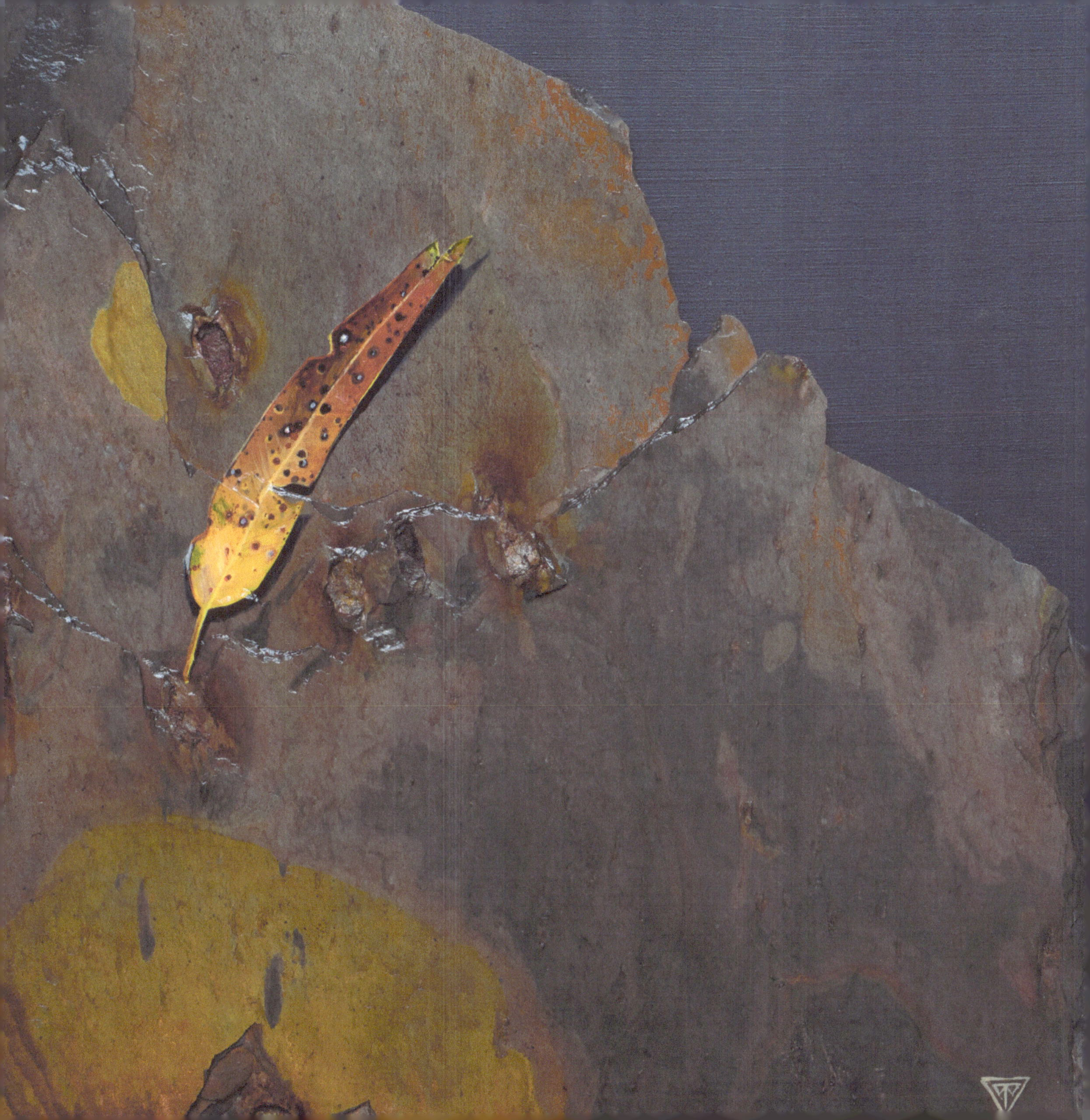

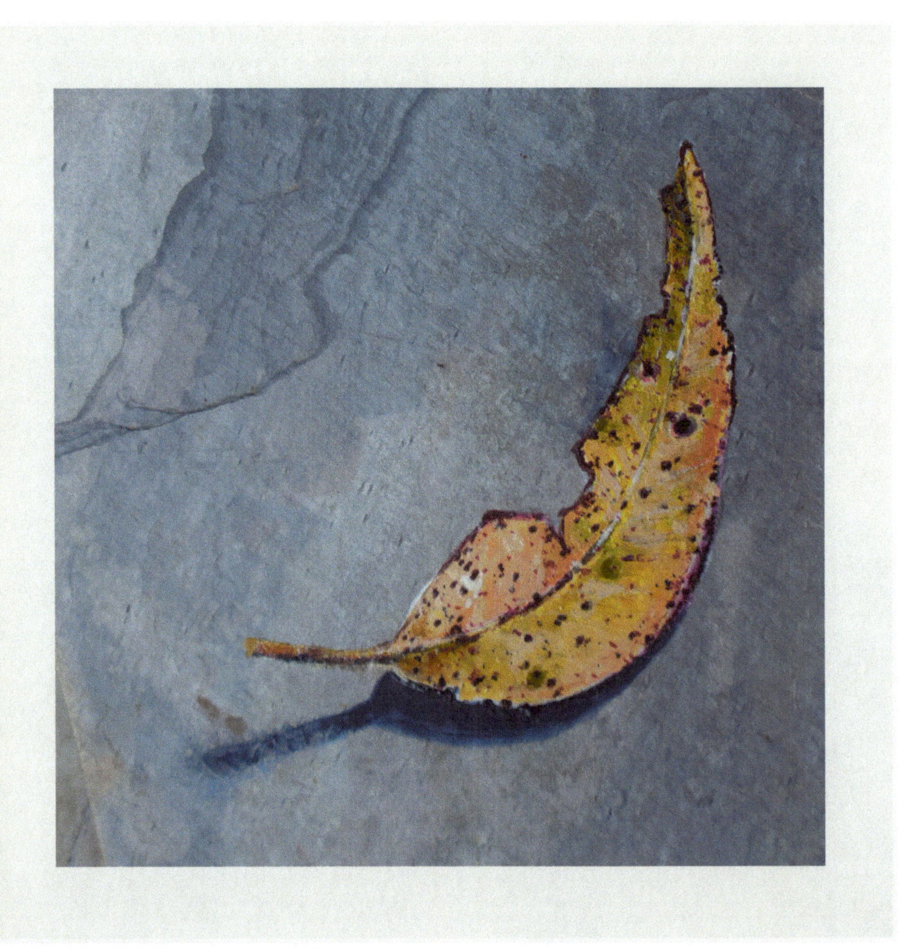

"What other people think of me,
is none of my business."

Ida Daly

Detail from *Pretty in pink*
28 x 13cm
Watercolour and gouache on paper

"When people ask if there was a common element in my experience of observing daily life in a wide range of cultures, I would reply: The poorest are usually the most generous, and the richest are the most reluctant to share their wealth."

John Tyman

"Old growth forest tree, you may be tall, stately, magnificent, but you would not exist without us millions of leaves; decaying, transforming, providing fertility."

Penny Watsford

Detail from *Equal Rights*
45 x 32cm
Watercolour and gouache on paper

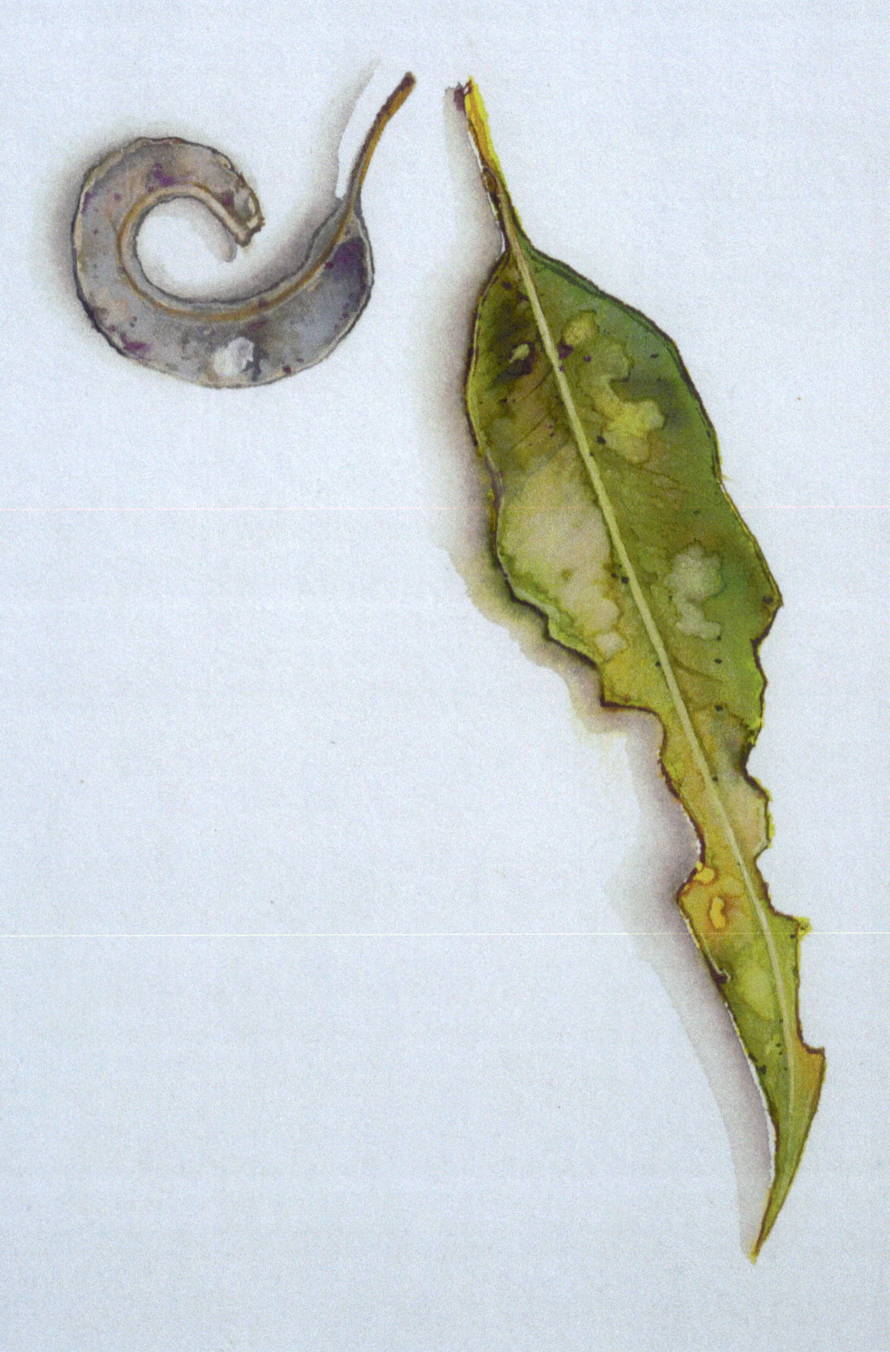

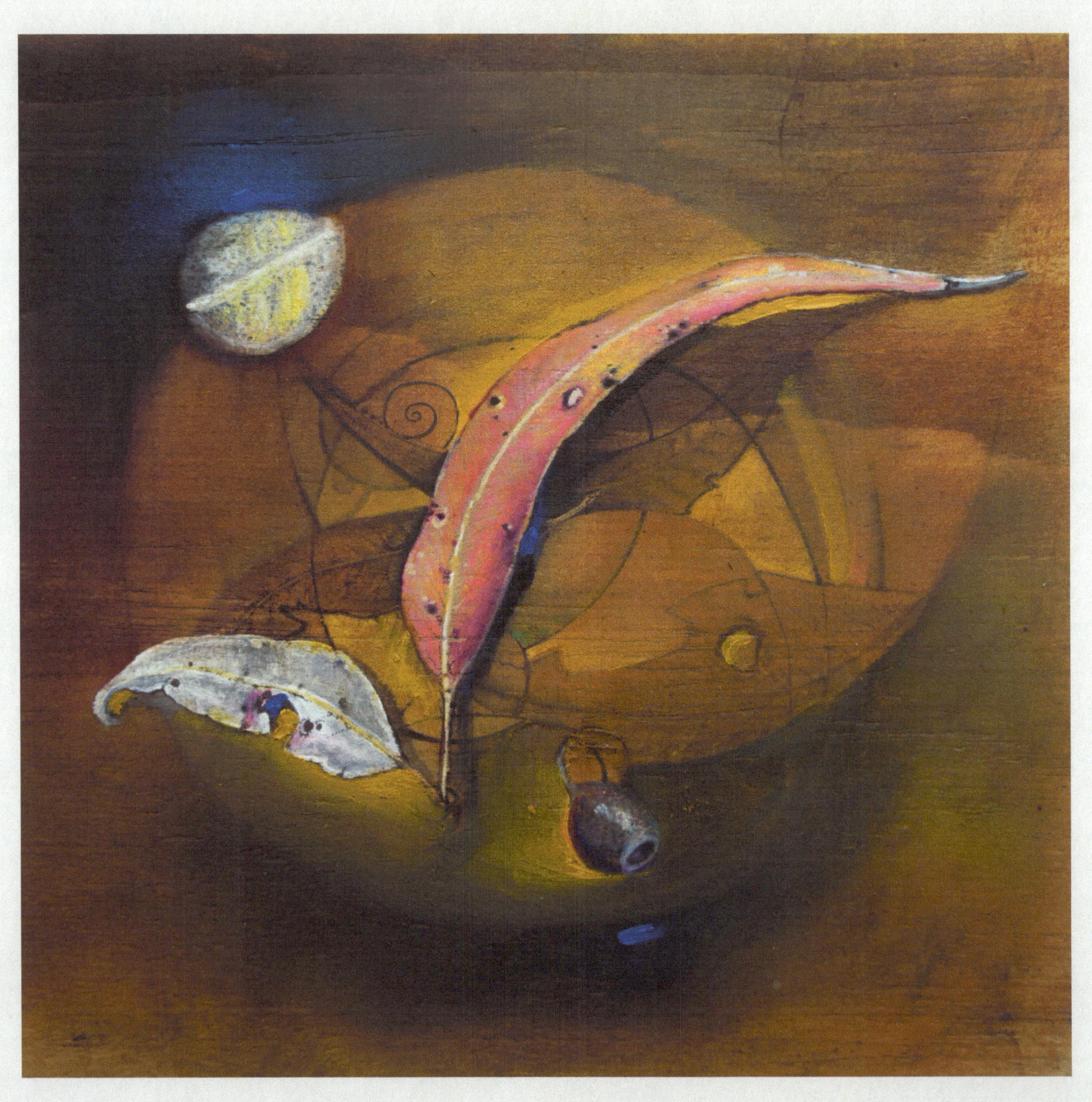

"Looking through the vertical window struts, past the dark, blurry, organic shapes of trees, onto the stars shining a million light years ago."

Madeleine Murray

Night
17 x 17cm
Oil, watercolour, acrylic and gouache on plywood

"What really lies hidden behind the veneer of our art – what fantasies, what desires? let's look together, let's look now."

David Kinneally

"We never expected to find ourselves at this time of our lives, in such a magic landscape, near a village full of vibrant and enthusiastic people. We love our life here."

Susan Kinneally

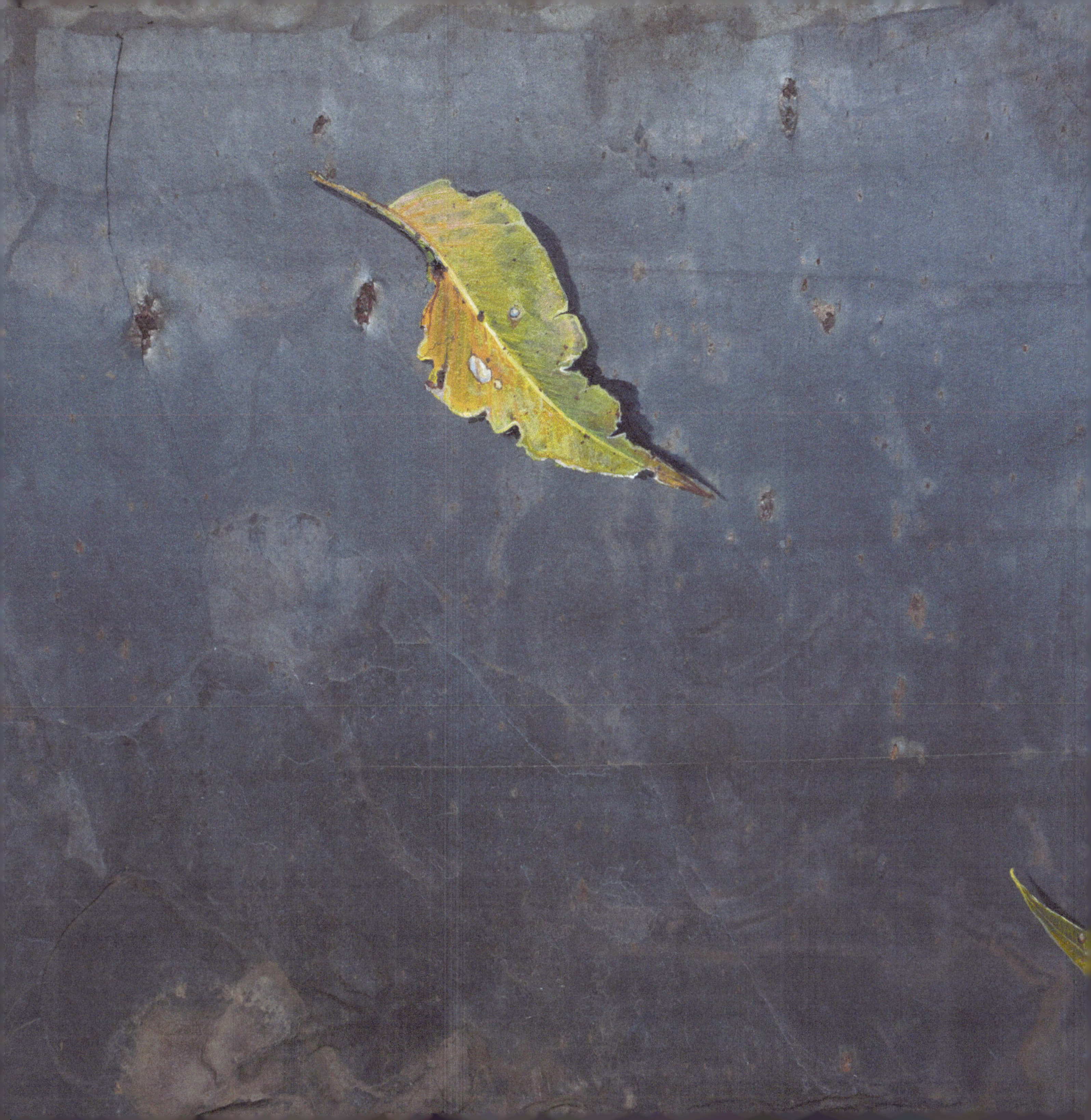

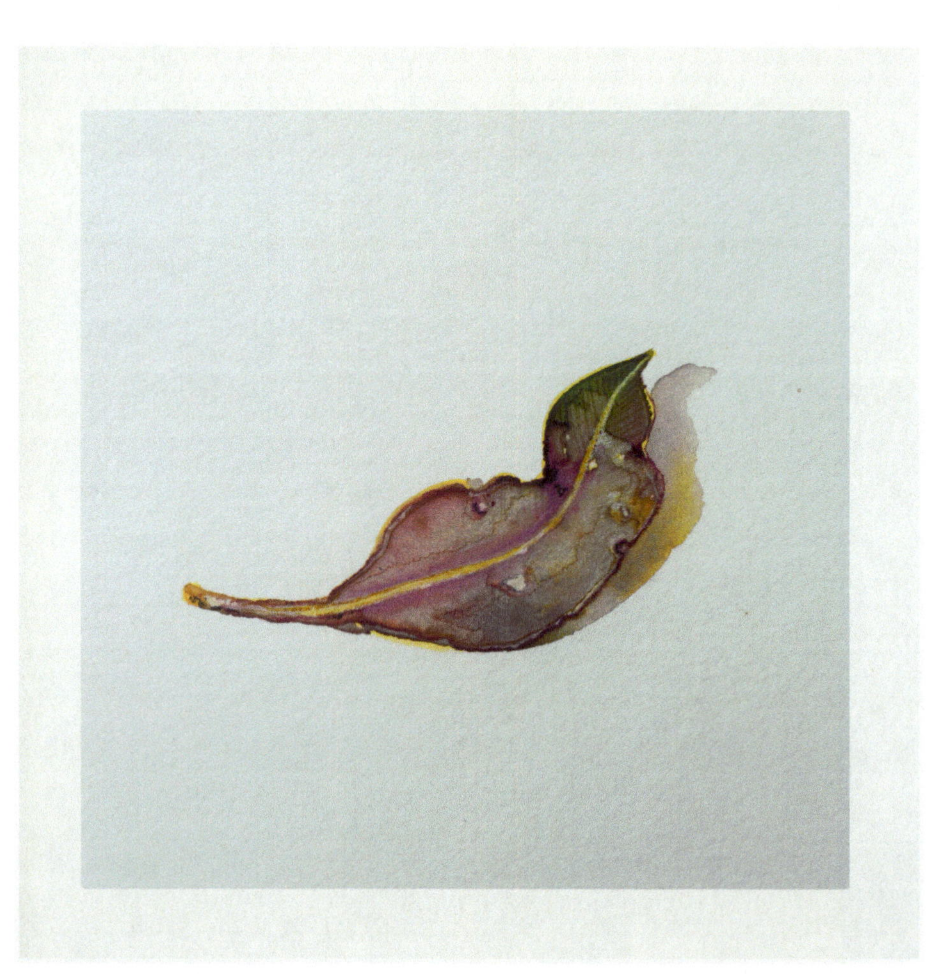

"Count it all joy."

Renae Quirk

Gratitude
11 x 11cm
Watercolour and gouache on paper

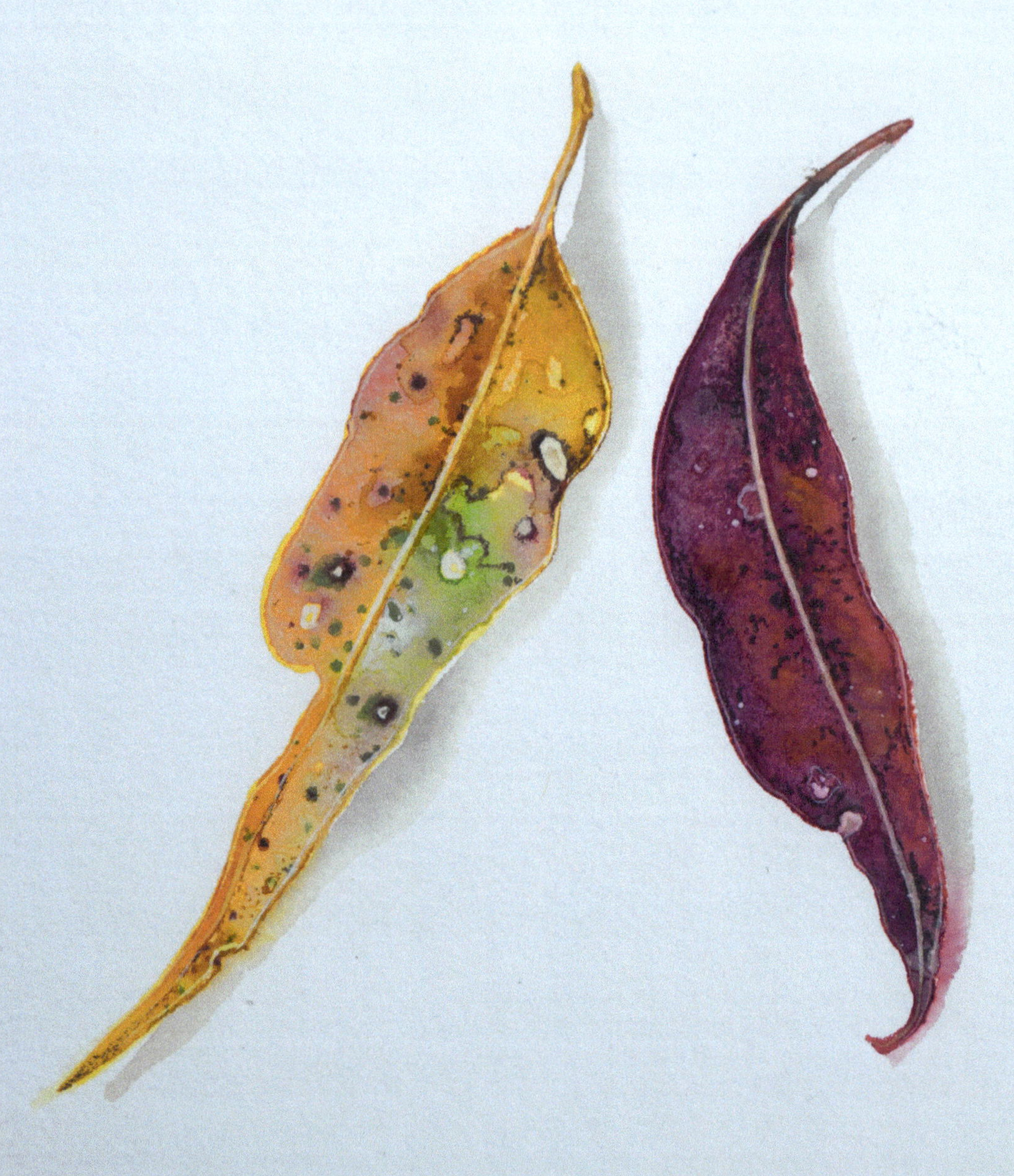

"Never be so busy as not to think of others."

Val Bell

Detail from *Not forgotten*
45 x 32cm
Watercolour and gouache on paper

"Happiness radiates like the fragrance from a flower
and draws all good things towards it."

Philippa Pierce

Happiness
11 x 11cm
Watercolour and gouache on paper

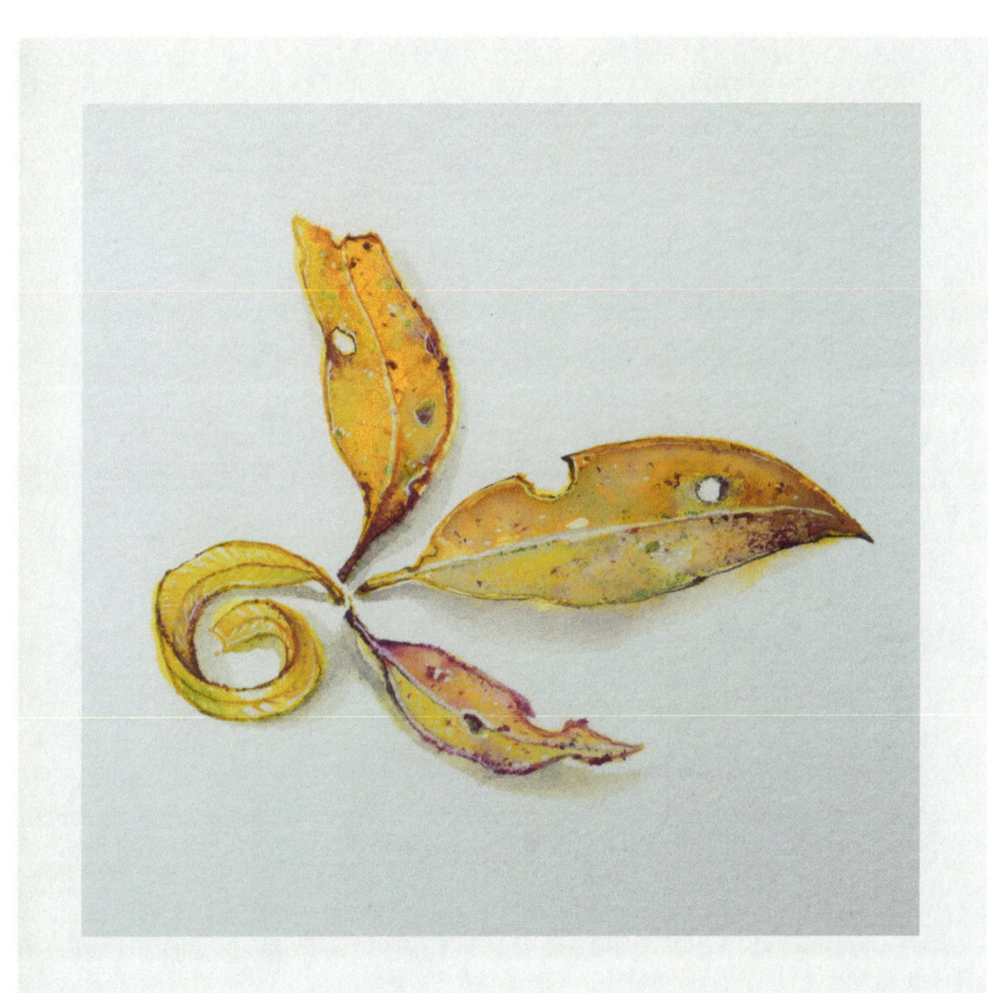

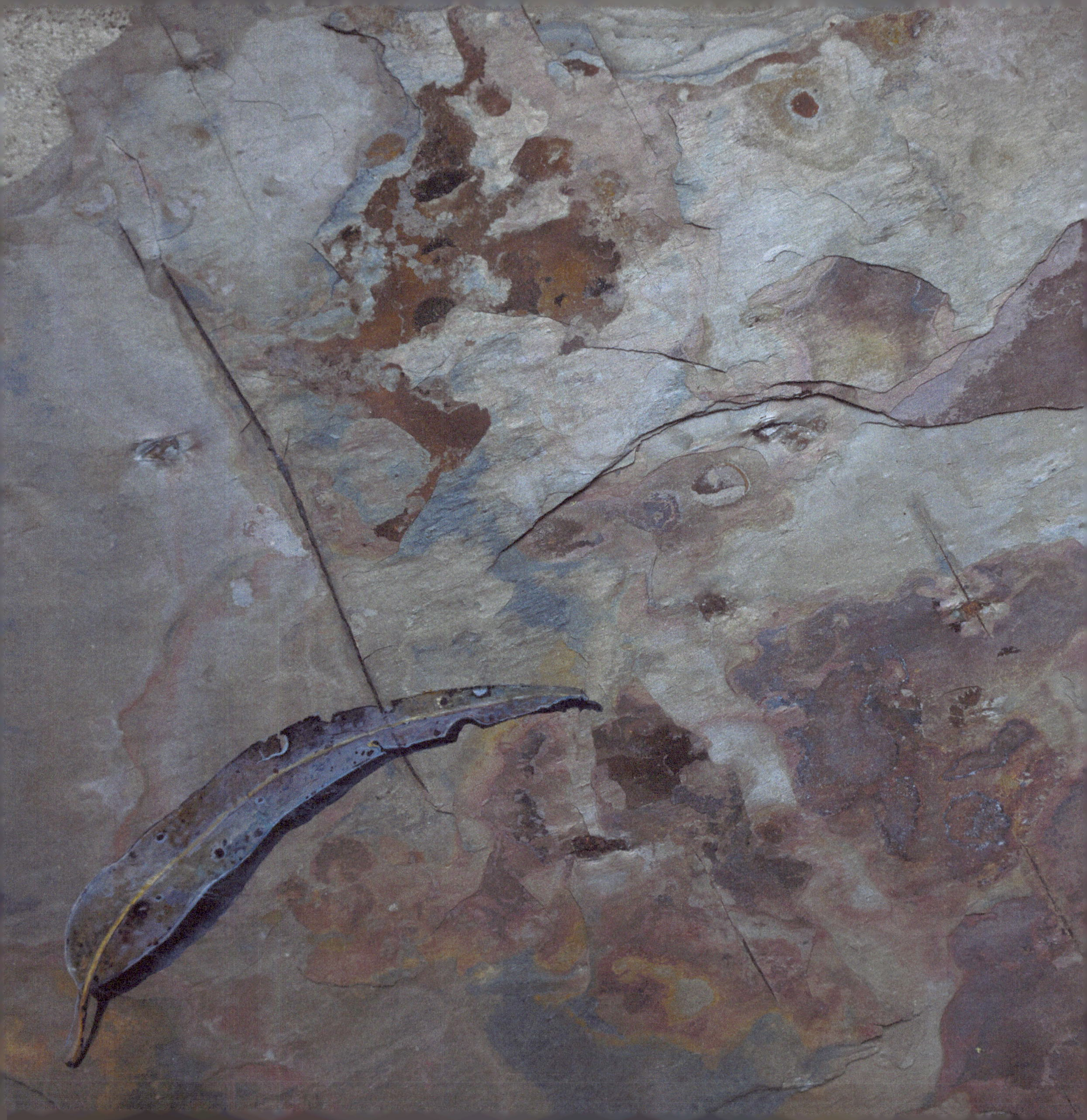

"The dreams have gone on ahead,
out of reach and almost out of sight."

Lisa Tiffen

"All leaves must fall."

Brian Bertram

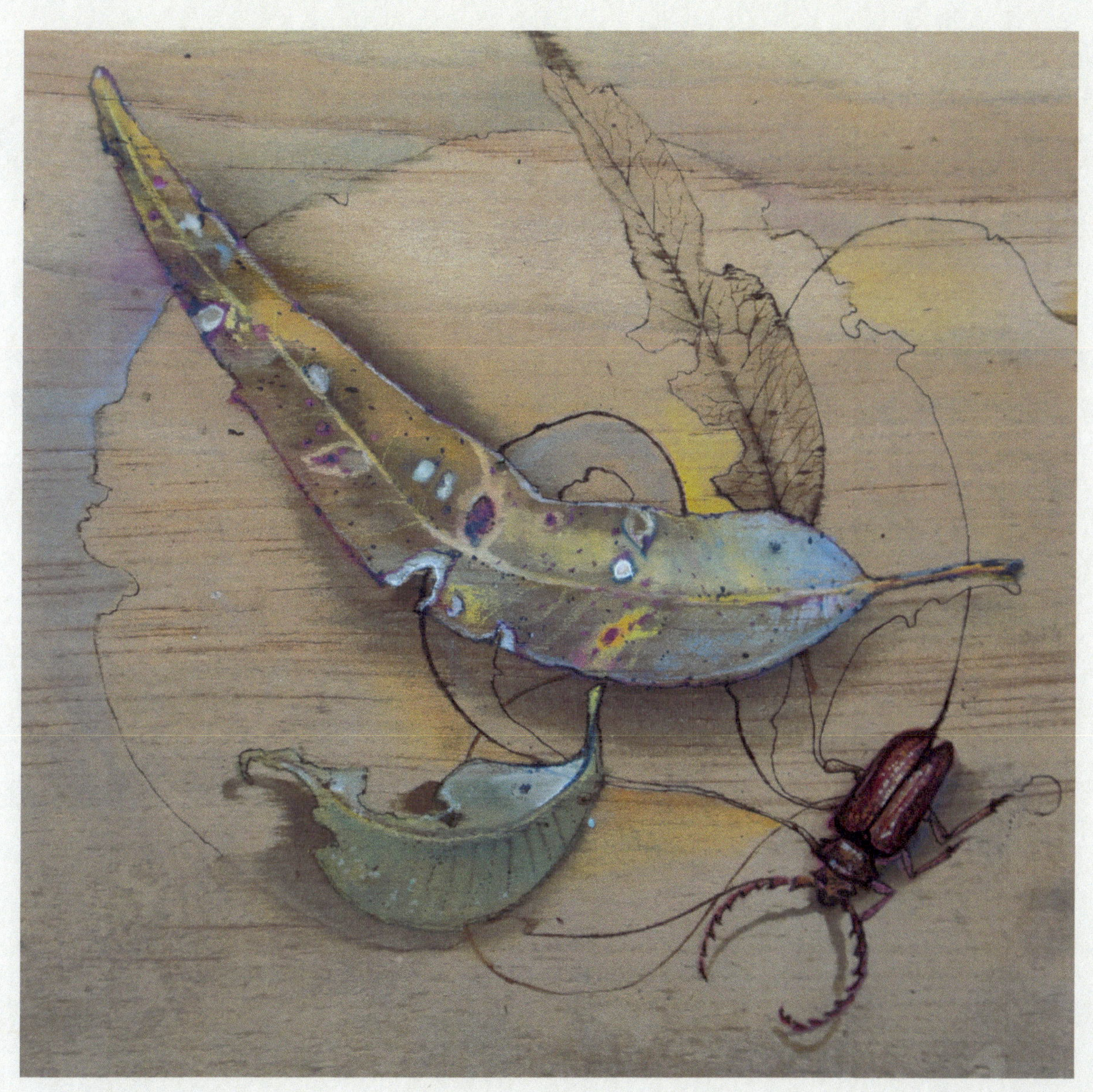

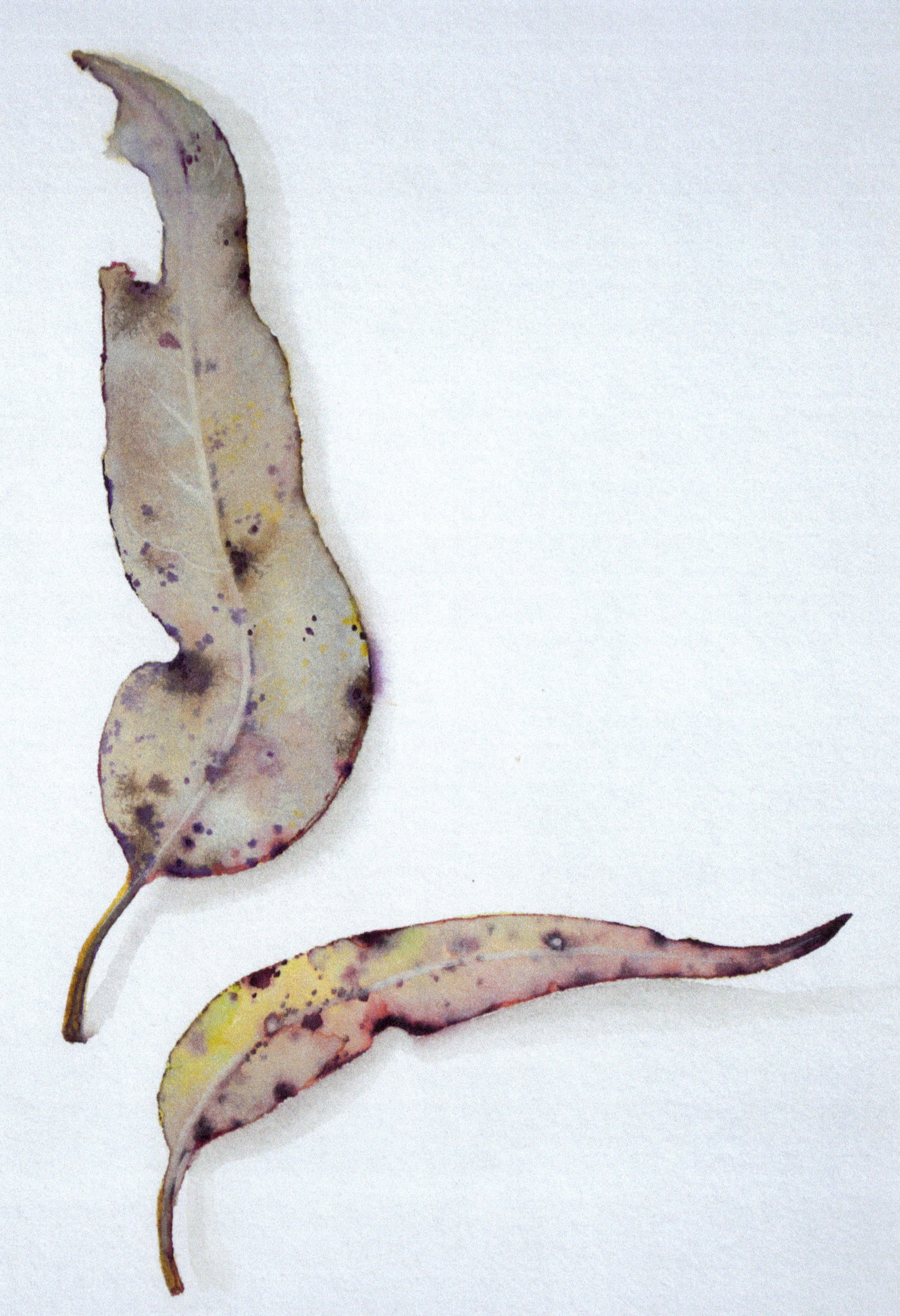

"A simulacrum on the lookout for a metaphysicist."

Sue Walston

Detail from *Watch over me*
45 x 32cm
Watercolour and gouache on paper

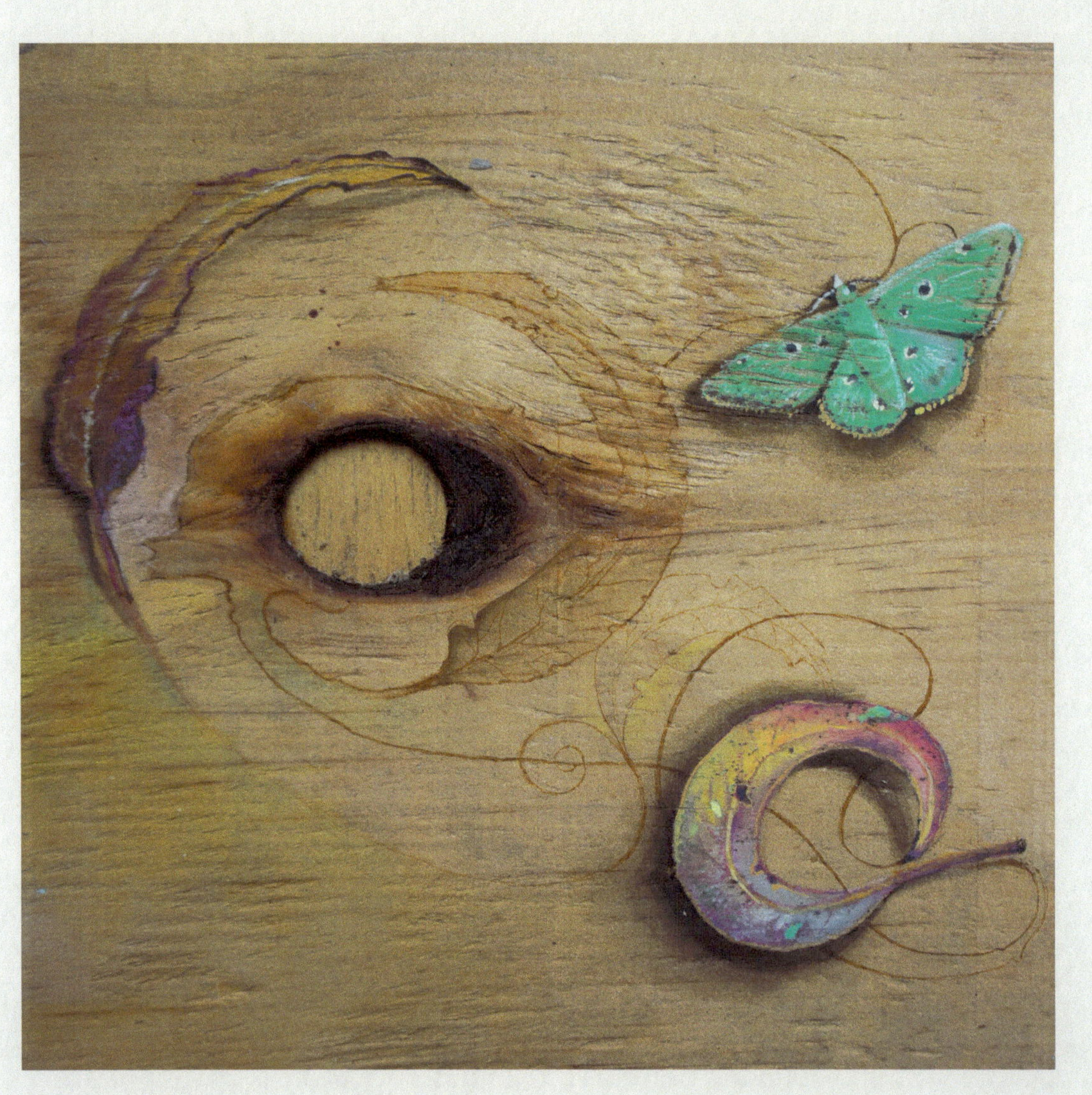

"Our withering creative urge can jolt back to life
when presented with a vibrant new image."

Denise Bell

Inspiration
17 x 17cm
Watercolour, ink and gouache on plywood

"Perfection is very, very elusive.
I need to always remind myself to be content with
something just a bit less."

Ken Rippin

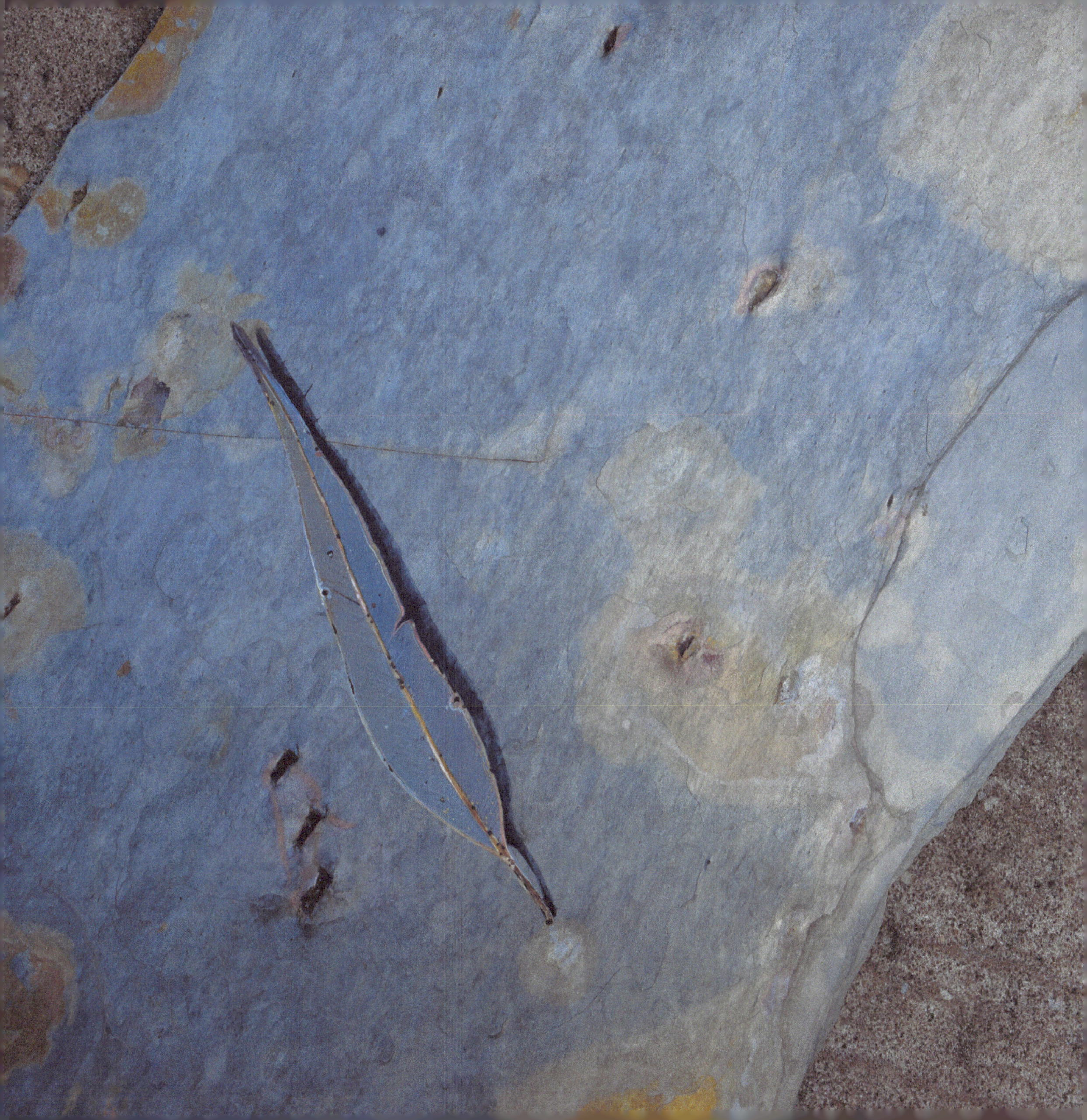

"Prostitutes could save the world."

Maya Krasna

Freedom
11 x 11cm
Watercolour and gouache on paper

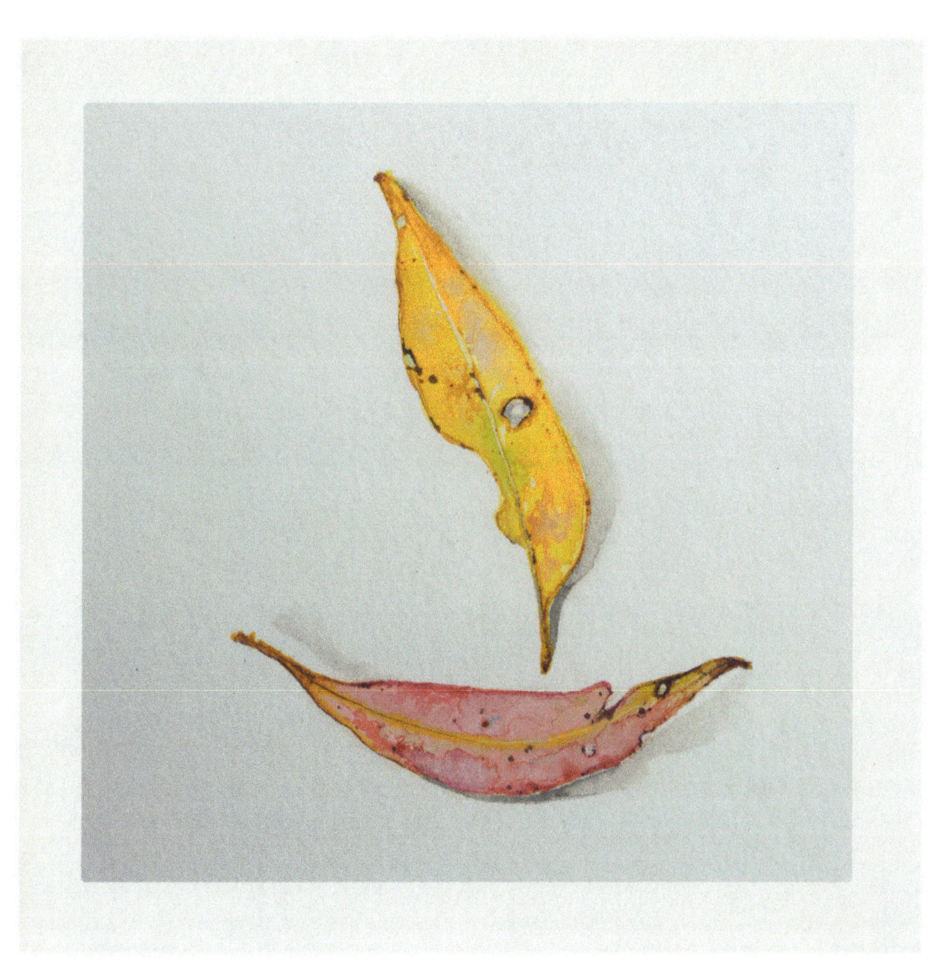

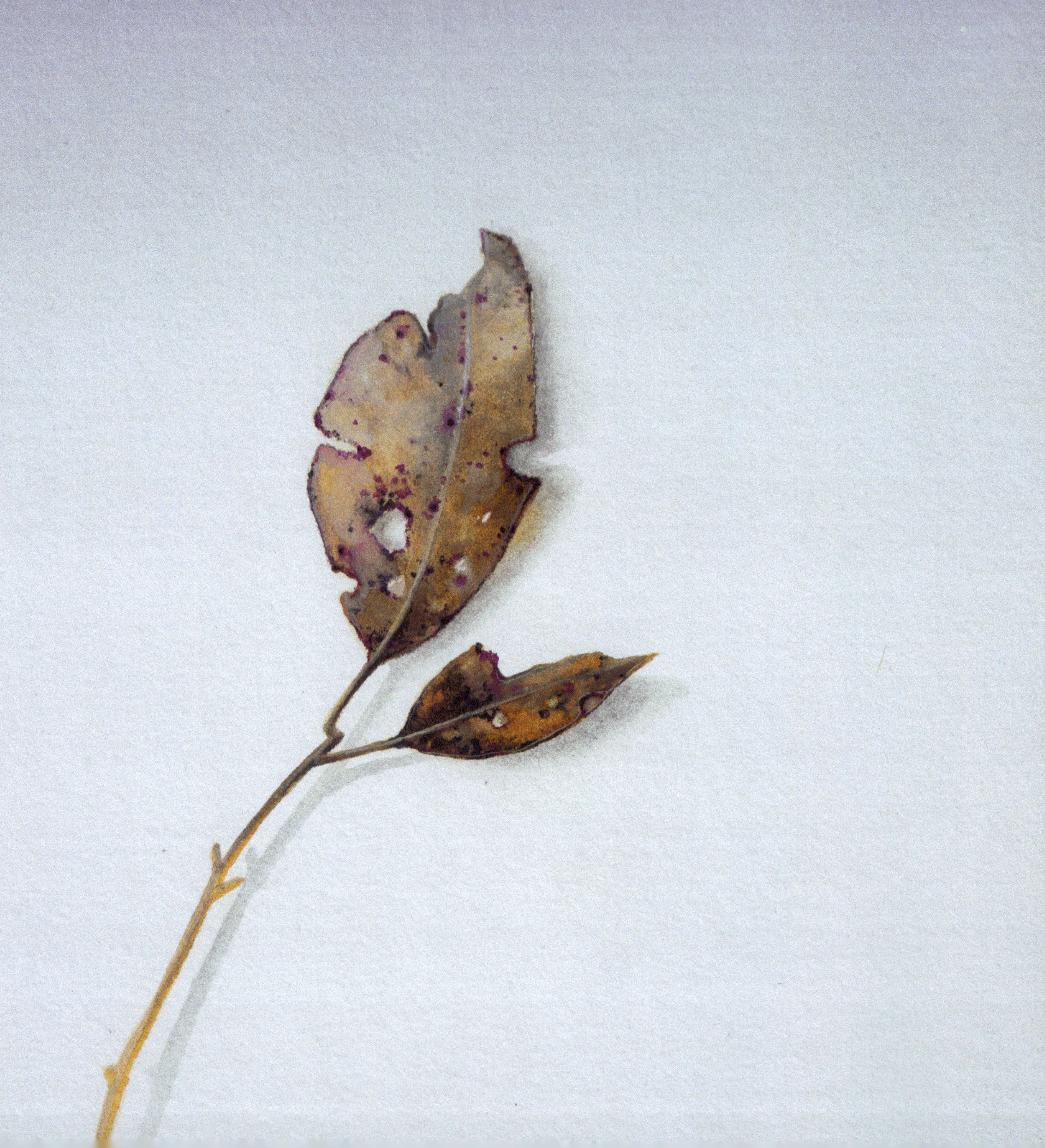

"Even foolhardy promises can be fulfilled if we fully accept our 'otherness' and allow the differences between us to flourish and nourish."

Heather and Bryan McClelland

Til death do us part
45 x 32cm
Watercolour and gouache on paper

"Joined at the Hip. Hip hip hooray!"

Trish Clark and Iain Finlay

Detail from *Peas in a Pod*
29 x 29cm
Acrylic and gouache on slate

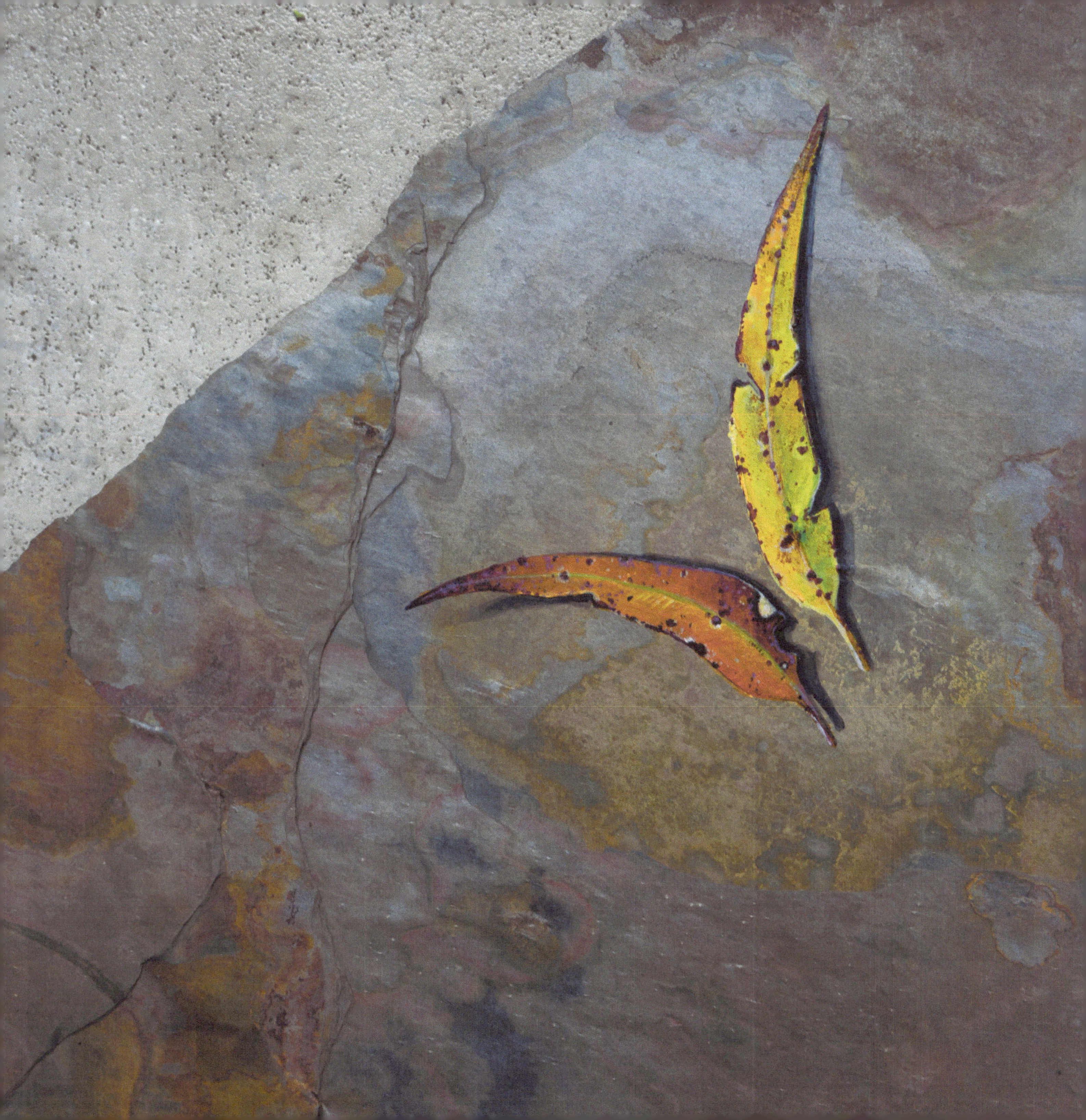

"It's not easy you know."

Judith Magee

On death
17 x 17cm
Watercolour, ink and gouache on plywood

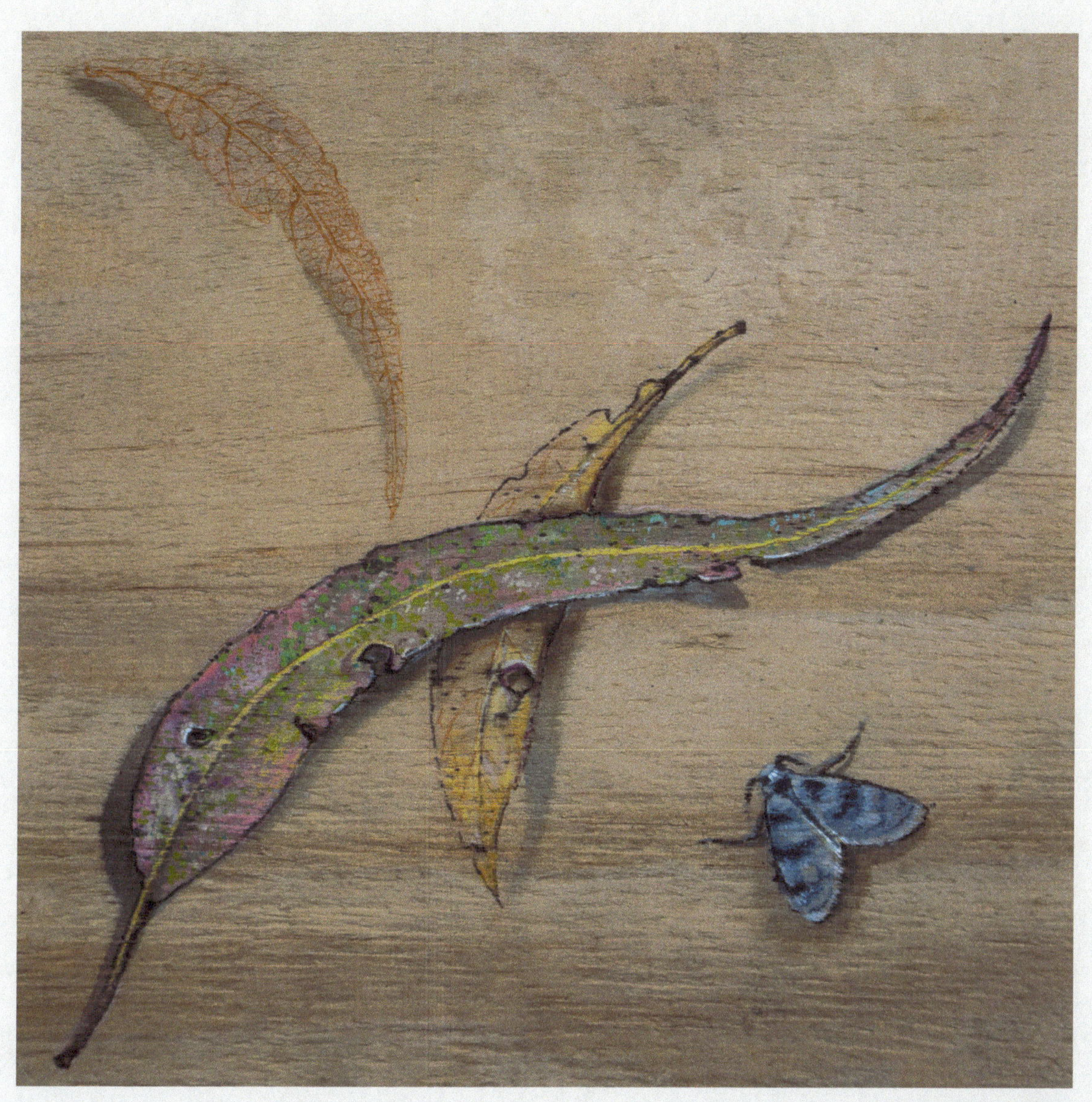

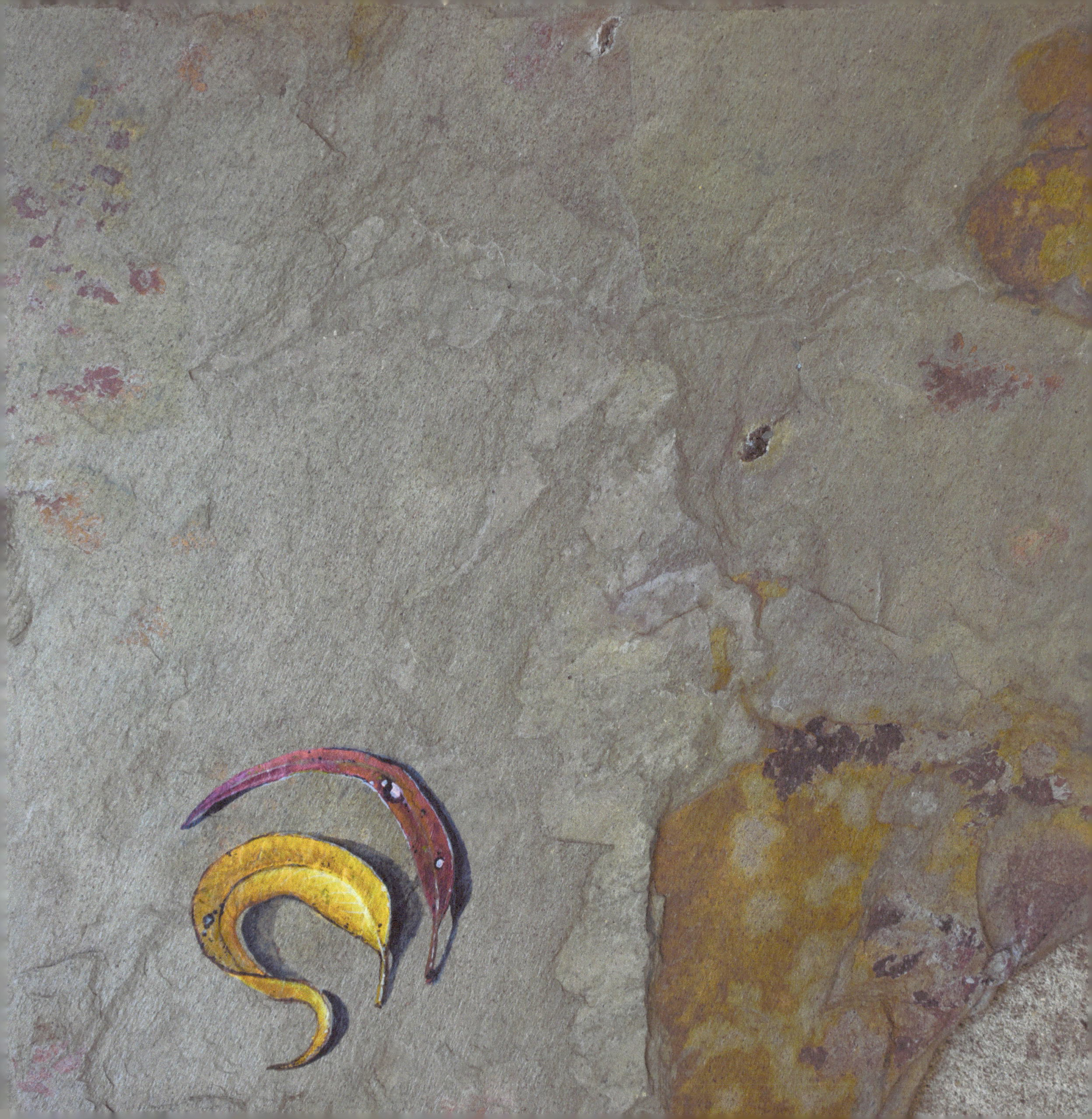

"Everything is going to be alright."

Julia Wunder

Nurture
29 x 29cm
Acrylic on slate

"The most enriching gift for us humans
is when we give."

Lenka Persi

Giving
11 x 11cm
Watercolour and gouache on paper

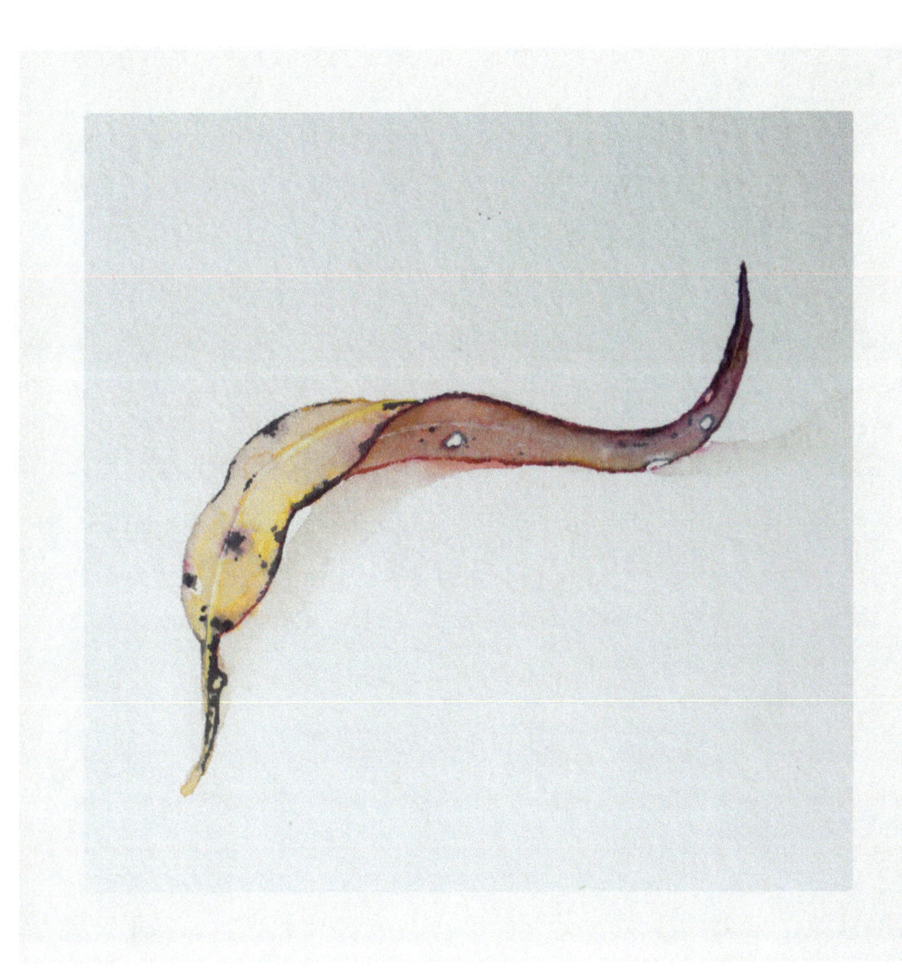

"Gratitude."

Holly and Richard Norton

Trust
29 x 29cm
Acrylic and watercolour on slate

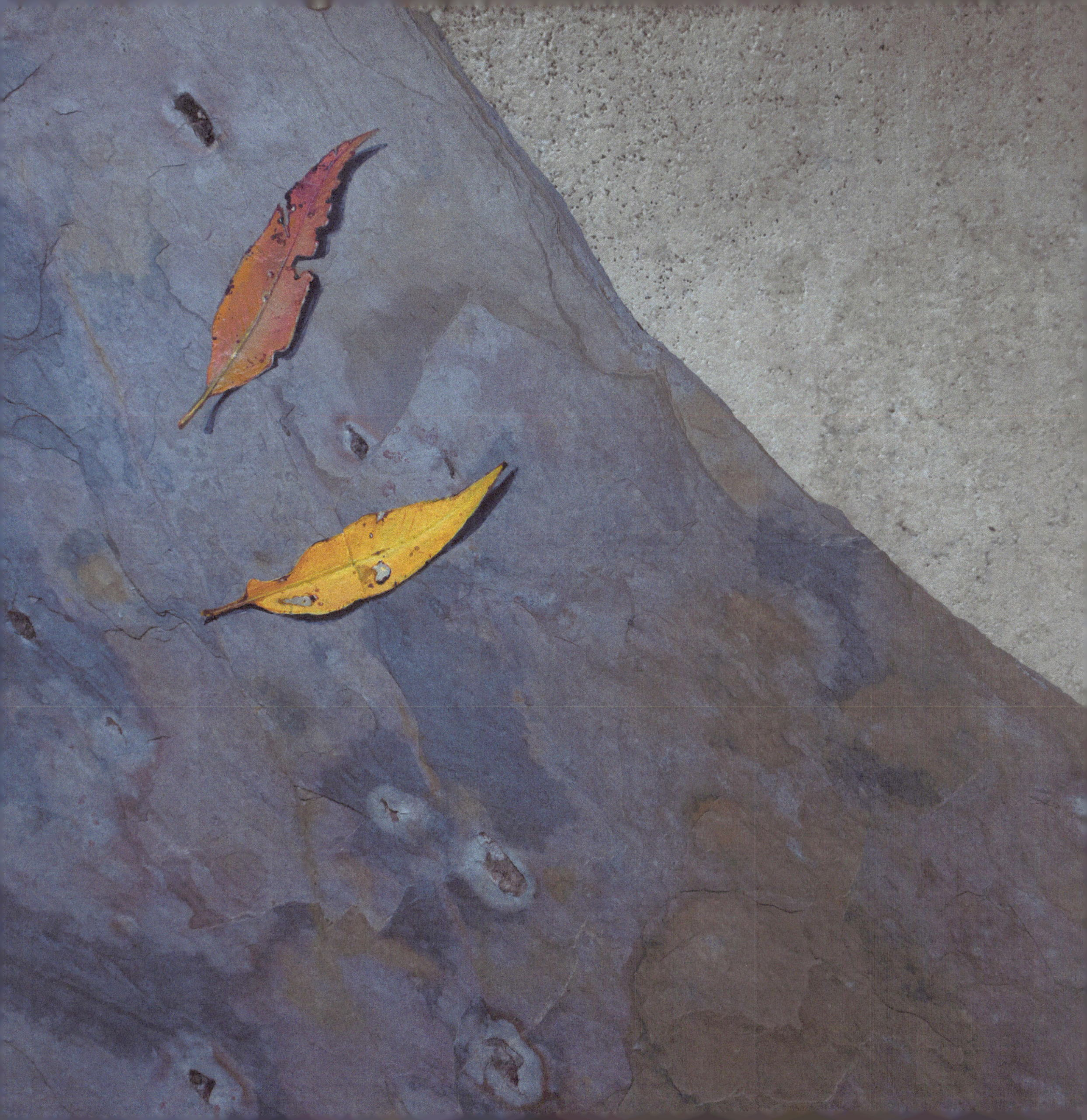

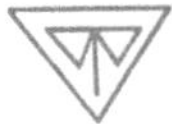

ABOUT THE ARTIST

Tina Wilson received a Bachelor of Arts (Visual Arts) from Newcastle University, majoring in Plant and Wildlife Illustration in 1996. She has worked as a visual artist and graphic designer across Australia for over 20 years.

While living in Perth and working as a graphic designer, Tina created Western Australia's very own national art prize – the Black Swan Prize for Portraiture. As its founder and executive director for ten years, she was delighted to see it grow into Australia's third richest portrait prize and the only one of its kind in WA.

In 2013 Tina was awarded the City of Perth Premier's Active Citizenship Award for her contribution to the arts. The Black Swan Prize for Portraiture is now proudly exhibited at the Art Gallery of Western Australia each year.

Following its success, Tina resigned in 2017 to return to her own creative practice.

Tina now lives with her partner in Uki, a small village in the Northern Rivers, NSW. She spends her time painting, drawing, writing, curating exhibitions and creating children's books.

You are welcome to contact Tina by email at
tinawilson@iinet.net.au

www.ingramcontent.com/pod-product-compliance
Lightning Source LLC
Chambersburg PA
CBHW042151030726

47599CB00004B/702